BEAUTIFUL DUCKS

PORTRAITS

of

CHAMPION
BREEDS

BEAUTIFUL DUCKS

PORTRAITS

of

CHAMPION BREEDS

by LIZ WRIGHT
photographed by ANDREW PERRIS

Ivy Press

First published in the UK in 2012

Ivy Press

210 High Street

Lewes

East Sussex BN7 2NS

United Kingdom

www.ivypress.co.uk

British Library Cataloguing-in-Publication Data
A catalogue record for this book is available from the British Library

ISBN: 978-1-908005-50-2

This book was conceived, designed and produced by

Ivy Press

Creative Director **Peter Bridgewater**
Publisher **Jason Hook**
Art Director **Wayne Blades**
Senior Editor **Jayne Ansell**
Designer **Ginny Zeal**
Photographer **Andrew Perris**
Photography Assistant **Anna Stevens**
Illustrator **David Anstey**

Printed in China
Colour Origination by Ivy Press Reprographics
9 8 7 6 5 4 3 2

CONTENTS

INTRODUCTION

It's a fascinating story how today's domestic duck transformed from being a wild bird – hunted by our ancestors for meat, then kept semi-feral on duck ponds – into the colourful and useful bird that lives closely with humankind the world over. With the exception of the MUSCOVY, all domestic ducks are believed to descend from the well-known Mallard; the multitude of these descendants is a tale of genetic mutation, selective breeding and the protective effects of domestication over the ages.

The wide-ranging nature of this variety is shown to you in *Beautiful Ducks*, in which show-bird specimens illustrate the very best examples of their kind. Each show-quality drake or duck has been spruced, washed and glossed for his or her moment in the limelight.

Photographing ducks is no easy task. Even though these show-stoppers have been well handled, ducks naturally want to move around and flap their wings. To do justice to their colour, their shape and their character, as the photographer has done in this collection, is an achievement worthy of some admiration.

Each superb photograph is complemented by comprehensive information on the breed's history, the qualities of that breed and what the ideal bird should look like – the Breed Standard being the ultimate guide for breeders and judges. There is also a note on the approximate size of the breed in question, on related breeds and on the bird's origin and current distribution.

In this book you will also learn about how enthusiasm for rearing ducks has flourished; how the utility duck of the 1800s became a show star; why passionate breeders of ducks were still developing new breeds as late as the 1980s; and why new colours of established breeds are continually being sought and shown.

Above: Ducks have come a long way from the well-known Mallard, as the designer ducks in this collection illustrate.

Ducks have a truly global history, from the very English AYLESBURY duck to the PEKIN duck from the East; from the HOOK BILL of Holland to the ROUEN of France; from the American CAYUGA to the SAXONY of Germany. These superb pictures of top-class international birds will show you ducks as you have never seen them before and are bound to provoke your interest in their history – and their future.

DUCKS IN CIVILIZATION

THE WILD DUCK HAS BEEN HUNTED THROUGHOUT history for its meat, although there is evidence that ducks were domesticated by the Romans and the Egyptians. There are records from the early Middle Ages of ducks being widely kept by abbeys and monasteries. These ducks, then as now, provided people with meat and with feathers for warm bedding. They also provided grease and fat, which were needed for cooking and sometimes for lighting.

The spread of ducks throughout the world was linked to the increase in trade between colonial countries from the seventeenth century onwards. The CALL duck, for example, came from the Far East to Holland via trading routes in the early nineteenth century, and was then used as a decoy duck in wildfowling. This practice soon spread to Britain.

The introduction of the railway also led to the increased spread of breeds. Eggs and ducklings could be transported with ease across counties and even across countries, and meat-ducks were brought into the cities, ending up on sale in butchers' shops and meat markets. The town of Aylesbury in

Above: Duck-herding is a common sight at agricultural shows, much to the delight of the crowd.

Buckinghamshire soon became the centre of duck production in England. Methods of breeding ducks in Aylesbury were incredibly unhygienic, however, and increasing concern about public hygiene finally put paid to these practices.

By then, the advent of the high-laying INDIAN RUNNER duck, which had reached Britain by Victorian times, had led to an increased interest in ducks as egg producers, rather than just as suppliers of meat.

By the time of the First World War duck breeders were concentrating on producing the 'ideal': a duck that provided meat, but also laid well, was calm and easy to keep and was also distinctive in appearance – the so-called utility duck.

The late twentieth century saw a further use for ducks as 'gardeners', with ducks being used in vineyards and in commercial growing to reduce the incidence of slugs and snails. And duck-herding by sheepdogs became part of agricultural displays. Today, ducks are still kept for their eggs, meat and feathers, but an increasing number of pure breeds are being kept for exhibition, too.

A BRIEF HISTORY OF SHOWING

THE VICTORIAN AGE SAW A RISE IN THE NUMBER OF agricultural shows. Traditional rural fairs had always been a place to meet and trade, but the fledgling Agricultural Societies introduced different classes for farm produce and animals, and late-nineteenth-century society in Britain, the United States and Australia entered the arena with enthusiasm. Duck-carcass classes in the dressed-poultry section were supplemented by live duck classes, in which the ducks' characteristics of productive value sat side-by-side with increasing curiosity among spectators about the newer imported breeds and about those being developed by breeders.

In June 1845 the first National Poultry Show for live birds was held at the London Zoological Gardens, and the exhibition world took off and flew. Breeders took great care in preparing their best specimens for show, and there was huge competition for the prestige that came with the top prizes. Very high prices were paid for show birds and for the new and unusual breeds that were now being imported from abroad. At the first American Poultry Show, which was held at Boston in 1849, 10,000 people visited, and the show had around 1,500 pens containing all types of poultry, including ducks.

Above: Since the Second World War, duck-showing has become a sport purely for hobbyists.

The popularity of duck-showing continued throughout the mid- to late nineteenth century, and increasing railway links assisted duck-keepers in this task, enabling the ducks to be picked up in their baskets, delivered to the show and then brought back in the evening – often while their owners stayed at home.

There were no shows during the Second World War, and the development of the commercial poultry industry in the 1950s meant that there were fewer small breeders and therefore fewer entrants to the shows. Gradually poultry shows became purely for hobbyists, and a new, different surge of enthusiasm for duck-keeping was seen – and remains to the present day. An increase in the number of top-quality breeders during the 1980s brought fresh life to the waterfowl scene and also led to the founding of specialized clubs for waterfowl breeds. And the popularity of some breeds, such as the CALL and the RUNNER, continued to promote the duck as a bird for exhibition.

THE BREED STANDARDS

ALTHOUGH POULTRY HAS BEEN KEPT (AND BREEDS developed) since the earliest historical records, the actual recording of a standard for each breed did not occur until the first Breed Standards were published in 1865 by the original Poultry Club. Four breeds of duck were defined: the CALL, the well-established AYLESBURY, the ROUEN and the popular BLACK EAST INDIAN. America followed with its own *Standards of Perfection* in 1867. The Waterfowl Club was founded in 1887 and played its part, too, in setting the Standards.

Over the years, as the clubs and associations amalgamated and sometimes re-formed to become the societies that we know today, more breeds were added and some of the Standards were refined. Individual breed clubs were formed for some, and a wealth of historical and current breeding knowledge was shared in order to formulate the Standards. Often the changes to the Standards were small and were introduced slowly, as it was felt important that the Standards should resist fashion 'fads' and continue to reflect the ducks' original purposes. A table bird, for example, should not suddenly be defined entirely by its colour, with its body shape being ignored.

The Standards define the ideal for the duck and drake, and give the optimum weights. The all-important Scale of Points sets out the number of points awarded to each feature, covering carriage, head, bill and neck, body, legs and feet, colour, size and condition. The maximum number of points available is 100, and how these can be awarded varies from breed to breed, according to the importance that is placed on particular features. For example, it is of vital importance that the true AYLESBURY has a flesh-pink-coloured bill, so this feature carries 25 points. Yet in a SILVER APPLEYARD the intricate plumage is more important, and 30 points can be awarded here; only 15 points are given for the head, bill and neck.

The Standards also state what would disqualify a breed, dividing these into main and minor faults. Ducks are classified as Light (mainly good egg-layers), Heavy (mainly table birds) and Bantams, and there are 23 standardized breeds. Some have several colour variations that have their own Standard.

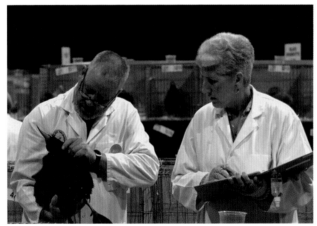

Above: Judges carefully consider each specimen according to the recommendations outlined in the Breed Standards.

BREEDS AND THEIR PURPOSES

I N ANCIENT HISTORY, DUCKS WERE HUNTED FOR THEIR meat, with their feathers providing a bonus for use in quilts. Their delicious eggs were also enjoyed, but it was not until the twentieth century – with the spread of the high egg-laying INDIAN RUNNER duck and its crosses – that duck eggs were produced on a commercial basis. This breed also brought their foraging skills from the rice fields of the Far East to help with pest clearance in gardens and vineyards. Today, ducks are kept for all these purposes, often fulfilling more than one task.

Some breeds, such as the CAMPBELL and the ABACOT RANGER, were developed as 'dual-purpose' birds – that is, for their meat and their eggs. Within the predominantly meat category comes the ROUEN, which was the archetypal French meat bird, although its vivid colouring and the impressive stature of the bird made it a natural choice for exhibitors. The AYLESBURY was the British equivalent, and since the first poultry shows in 1845 it has found a natural home on the show bench. Penguin-like in its stance, the PEKIN is the Eastern meat duck and has been crossed into many

breeds to produce commercial table ducks, but is seen as a statuesque pure breed at shows.

The CAMPBELL has not been surpassed as an egg producer, and is used as such to this day, but it was the INDIAN RUNNER that, when imported to Britain, became hugely influential on egg-laying breeds of ducks; in 1918 it was termed the 'egg and land duck *par excellence*'.

In the last 100 years or so, even for successful egg-producing and table birds, the magnificent plumage and impressive shape of some breeds has made them attractive to breeders and exhibitors. The 1980s saw an increase in the development of new breeds for the show pens, such as the MINIATURE SILVER APPLEYARD and the MINIATURE CRESTED – perhaps the first time that a duck has been specifically 'designed' for exhibition, although they are still handy egg-layers, reverting to their productive roots.

Pet ducks, too, are popular this century, and the CALL – with its big eyes, small stature and friendly personality – has certainly found its niche in this respect, as well as being outstandingly popular with breeders and with judges on the show bench.

Above: Throughout history, ducks have been used for their succulent meat, their soft feathers and their delicious eggs.

CARING FOR DUCKS

ALL DUCKS, WHETHER THEY ARE STARS OF THE show bench, pet ducks or egg-layers, have the same basic requirements for their care. They are classified as waterfowl and, as such, need access to water. It does not have to be a lake, but they must at least have a splashing pool, for all ducks must be able to get their heads and necks fully immersed in water and also need to splash in order to activate their preening gland – this is essential to keep their plumage in good order. There is also an emotional need for ducks to interact with water.

They require balanced nutrition, usually in the form of ready-mixed duck pellets. People who show exhibition ducks tend to have their own 'secret' recipes and supplements, to get the optimum sheen on their feathers, or the eyes extra-bright.

In addition, ducks need to be kept as clean as possible – they are not nature's cleanest birds and can soon turn a duck pen or run into a soupy, muddy mess. They therefore need a pen that has a dry floor (at least initially) and a well-maintained run with access to water. Many breeds also thrive if they have a larger area, such as an orchard, for foraging.

Above: All waterfowl, including ducks kept for showing, need access to water in order to keep their plumage in good order.

Finally, ducks need to be protected from predators of all kinds. The fox is the most persistent and potentially damaging predator, but domestic dogs can also take their toll, as can mink. Ducklings are in danger from smaller mammals, such as rats or stoats, as well as being vulnerable to attack from the skies, in the form of hawks.

Ducks and drakes that are selected for exhibition need to have their feathers in tip-top condition, so they are kept away from the breeding pen while they are being shown, as the rough-and-tumble of mating would damage their all-important neck plumage. Some breeds should also be kept away from bright sunlight, as this may fade the colour of their feathers.

A star bird needs carefully designed accommodation that will keep it protected and clean, while enabling it to behave naturally: splashing in water and foraging in the earth. Show birds will also need 'pen training' – that is, handling regularly so that they are calm when being judged, and while being kept in a smaller pen for a day or more at the show. They will also need to get used to being bathed for the big day.

CHAMPIONSHIP SHOWS

A T THE VERY TOP OF THE SHOW TREE ARE THE National Championship Shows, where you will see the very finest ducks. All countries have some form of these shows.

Below these come the Championship Shows, recognized as the main shows in a particular area. The status of these shows is regularly reassessed. There are special prize cards for the Best in Show, Reserve and the Main Section winners. Regional Shows were introduced in 1977, and again have special awards and prestige. And then there are Voucher Shows, where a show affiliated to the Poultry Club of Great Britain is entitled to offer Voucher Cards for, among other sections, Best Waterfowl. These arenas represent the 'grass roots' of showing, and provide novices with the opportunity to start showing and gain confidence.

Whether being exhibited at a national or local show, all show-quality ducks undergo rigorous preparation. They must first have had sufficient pen training. They must be tame enough to be handled and to cope with the 'bright lights' of the show world. Ducks must also be spotlessly clean. Bathing is often done a

Above: Show ducks require rigorous preparation in order to have a chance at becoming a prize-winning champion.

few days before the show, for best results, but the feet, legs and bill usually require attention on the day. Ducks must also be free of external parasites. A 'show kit', comprising soapy water, brush, towel and maybe some oil, is usually taken to the show. On arrival, pen numbers are given out and the ducks are put in their allocated pens to await judging.

The judge is accompanied by a steward, who carries the paperwork and notes down the judge's decision; he or she also carries a copy of the Breed Standards for reference. The ducks sport merely a pen number, and their owners are normally excluded during the judging process. The judge begins by assessing the duck in its pen, and is then likely to take the bird from the pen for closer scrutiny. The judge is not comparing the duck to others in the class, but to the Breed Standard, to see how it marks. After judging the individual class (such as Best AYLESBURY), the Best Waterfowl is selected from all the winners and placed in a row of pens called 'Championship Row'. From these champions, an overall Best in Show is selected.

THE DUCKS

Getting one's *ducks in a row* can present a challenge, but we have lined up 40 IMPRESSIVE MODELS for you, including delightfully *diminutive drakes*, devastating DESIGNER DUCKS, and a whole raft of BEST-IN-CREST show-stopping, high-laying, tall-standing, *wonderful waterfowl.*

INDIAN RUNNER

AMERICAN FAWN & WHITE DRAKE

Although the INDIAN RUNNER is normally known for its distinctive carriage, back in the early 1900s it was the bird's impressive egg-laying performance that got people talking. The writer E. A. Taylor wrote of Runner ducks in 1918: 'it will be stocked in preference to the hen'. Today Runners are a stalwart of the show bench, appearing in all colours, but always identifiable by their upright carriage and elegant appearance.

Features

The Indian Runner can look almost perpendicular if it is interested, alarmed or has been trained to do so. The alert eyes are set very high in the head, above a long, slender neck. The body is sometimes described as 'bottle-shaped', with the legs set well back to maintain the upright carriage.

Use

Standardized in 1901, with other colours added over the years, the Indian Runner has long been prized by breeders. Its range of colours and eye-catching stance make it a naturally flamboyant duck at exhibition. It is also a prolific egg-layer and its genes formed part of many utility ducks in the early twentieth century.

Related Breeds

The Runner is related to the Bali – another duck with an upright carriage. It has also been used in the development of the Abacot Ranger, Orpington, Khaki Campbell and Welsh Harlequin.

Size

Drake .... 1.6–2.3 kg (3½–5 lb)

Duck .... 1.4–2 kg (3–4½ lb)

Origin and Distribution

Introduced into Britain from Malaya in the nineteenth century, the Indian Runner is now well established in Europe, the USA and Australia.

Malaya

ORPINGTON
BUFF DUCK

The famous breeder of the Orpington chicken, William Cook, developed the ORPINGTON duck at his Kent farm. It was first advertised in 1910 as a breed that combined beauty with table qualities and profitable egg-laying, but found its way onto the show bench soon afterwards. Trying to breed Orpingtons with a consistently uniform shade is a challenge for breeders.

Features

Orpingtons are energetic, but should not appear excessively upright in carriage. The drake should have a head and neck that are a darker shade than the body, but with no hint of a green sheen. The duck (shown here) should show an even colour of buff, with no blue, brown or white feathers or any pencilling. Both should have alert brown eyes and orange-red legs.

Uses

This is the duck version of the Orpington chicken, and was renowned in its time as both a meat and an egg bird. In 1946 it was described as 'a general purpose bird, combining beauty with table qualities and profitable egg production'. Today, however, these attractive ducks are kept for show.

Related Breeds

William Cook did not share his secret, but it is generally thought this breed was developed by crossing Indian Runners with Aylesburys, Rouens and Cayugas.

Size

Drake .... 2.2–3.4 kg (5–7½ lb)

Duck .... 2.2–3.2 kg (5–7 lb)

Origin and Distribution

Originating in the English town of Orpington in Kent during the late nineteenth century, the Orpington is now found throughout Britain and Europe and in the USA. It is recognized by the American Livestock Conservancy as being a 'Threatened' breed.

England

ABACOT RANGER

DRAKE

Originating in Colchester, Essex, and named after the farm where it was bred, the ABACOT RANGER is a good egg-layer and an acceptable table bird. Created in 1917, it almost died out in Britain and was standardized first in Germany in 1934. It was not until 1987 that it was standardized in Britain. It is a very striking duck, with a distinctive 'hood', and is an active forager.

Features

The Abacot Ranger was originally known as the 'Hooded Ranger', the hood being its distinguishing feature. The drake (shown here) has a black head with a strong green lustre, divided from the rest of the plumage by a distinctive silver neck ring; the duck is fawn, with a darker shade of head and neck. The plumage is tight and glossy. It has an alert, upright body stance.

Use

Bred as a utility duck, the Abacot Ranger is a useful layer of up to 250 eggs a year, while providing meat for the table. It is an avid forager and, given a good range, can find a proportion of its own food. With their eye-catching colours, Abacot Rangers are striking exhibition birds.

Related Breeds

It is believed that this bird derives from cross-breeding Khaki Campbells and White Indian Runners, both of which lend their productive qualities to the Abacot Ranger.

Size

Drake .... 2.3–2.5 kg (5–5½ lb)

Duck .... 2–2.3 kg (4½–5 lb)

Origin and Distribution

The breed originated in England, but was imported into Germany in 1926, where it was enthusiastically developed, even though numbers became very low in its home country. Although still not common in the UK, it is kept by admirers across Europe.

England

MUSCOVY
CHOCOLATE DUCK

Often known as 'the Marmite duck' – because it is either loved or loathed for its unusual appearance, strong personality and determination to fly – the Muscovy is now a regular in show pens across the world, where a range of colours has gradually been developed. Unusually among domestic ducks, the drake is twice the size of the duck and also has more pronounced caruncles.

Features

Everything about this bird is powerful, from its personality to its long, strong body and the pronounced, fleshy caruncles on the face. As expected in a perching duck, the Muscovy has toenails on its capable feet. The Chocolate Muscovy (shown here) must show an even shade of chocolate, apart from a permissible patch of white on the wing coverts.

Use

Although the Muscovy is now a colourful visitor to shows around the globe, it has been kept since early history for its meat and large white eggs. Being able to forage for food and efficiently raise large families of ducklings also made the hardy Muscovy particularly attractive as a domestic duck.

Related Breeds

The Muscovy is a unique breed, for it is the only domestic duck that does not have the Mallard as a common ancestor.

Size

Drake .... 4.5–6.3 kg (10–14 lb)

Duck .... 2.3–3.2 kg (5–7 lb)

Origin and Distribution

Now found throughout the world, having been spread via trade routes and more deliberately by enthusiasts, the Muscovy originated in South and Central America. It is standardized in the USA, Australia and Europe.

South & Central America

INDIAN RUNNER
WHITE DRAKE

It is the carriage of this eye-catching duck that fascinates the viewer: when standing fully alert, the INDIAN RUNNER displays a straight line from the back of the head to the tip of the tail. But it also changed the perception of ducks when it was introduced, for this breed was found to lay far more eggs than any duck previously known. Some duck-keepers thought it would even replace the chicken as the top egg-laying bird.

Features

The duck is very long in appearance, with a slim, elegant neck that accounts for at least one-third of its length. The well set-back legs enable the Indian Runner to move at speed and cover considerable ground in a day. The White (shown here) was first standardized in 1922 and has sky-blue eyes and an orange bill and feet, which stand out from the tight, pure-white plumage.

Use

The Indian Runner is a natural show bird, with its alert nature and stunning features. It also has a unique flocking ability, which is used in sheepdog demonstrations. In the early twentieth century the Indian Runner could outclass most egg-laying hens of the time.

Related Breeds

The Indian Runner is closely related to the Bali. In the twentieth century crosses with the Indian Runner produced the Abacot Ranger, Khaki Campbell, Orpington and Welsh Harlequin.

Size

Drake .... 1.6–2.3 kg (3½–5 lb)

Duck .... 1.4–2 kg (3–4½ lb)

Origin and Distribution

The Indian Runner originated in Malaya, where stone carvings show it was established more than 1,000 years ago. It was imported into Britain in the 1830s and is now popular worldwide, being shown by enthusiasts in the USA, Australia and Holland.

Malaya

AYLESBURY

DUCK

The archetypal farmyard duck, the AYLESBURY played a vital role in the development of the English town that gave it its name. Bred as a meat bird, on one night alone in 1850 one ton of six- to eight-week-old ducklings was taken from Aylesbury by rail to London. It was one of the first birds to have its own class in early poultry shows, where weight was valued as highly as type.

Features

The true Aylesbury has a flesh-pink bill – the importance of which is underlined by the head, neck and bill category carrying 25 points out of the 100 available in the Breed Standard. It should have a horizontal carriage and a deep, broad body supported by strong orange legs. The only colour is the distinctive white plumage, which is said to resemble satin in appearance.

Use

With its pale skin and large body, the Aylesbury was a meat bird through and through, although the white feathers were also used for quilts and pillows. It was bred in its thousands by 'duckers' from the town of Aylesbury in the nineteenth century, with many people rearing ducklings inside their cottages.

Related Breeds

A true breed, the Aylesbury has no relations. The Pekin, another impressive table bird, was imported to Britain in the late nineteenth century and often crossed with it, meaning that the true Aylesbury became much harder to find.

Size

Drake .... 4.5–5.4 kg (10–12 lb)

Duck .... 4.1–5 kg (9–11 lb)

Origin and Distribution

This duck was developed in Aylesbury in Buckinghamshire, England, and was standardized in 1865. It spread throughout the world and is a top exhibition bird. It is in the 'Critical' category with the American Livestock Conservancy.

England

MAGPIE
DUN & WHITE DUCK

A strikingly marked duck, the MAGPIE had been seen on small farms in west Wales for some years prior to its development as a recognized breed. This bird was eventually standardized in 1926, and further colours in addition to the original 'magpie black-and-white' have now been developed, although breeding ducks with evenly matched markings is a constant challenge.

Features

The symmetry of the Magpie's markings is all-important, with nearly one-third of the total marks being awarded for colour. All birds show a 'cap' on the head and are disqualified if they do not have one. Originally found in black and white, the Magpie is now bred in blue and white, chocolate and white, and dun and white (shown here) and has a strong, active body.

Use

The Magpie is a very good layer, of mainly white (sometimes blue or green) good-sized eggs. It also has a good carcass, making it an acceptable table bird. It is very alert and can find some of its own food in a free-range setting, making it a useful breed for smallholders and in orchards.

Related Breeds

The Magpie is a unique breed of duck and has no relations.

Size

Drake .... 2.5–3.2 kg (5½–7 lb)

Duck .... 2–2.7 kg (4½–6 lb)

Origin and Distribution

This duck is firmly rooted in the farmsteads of Wales and was first standardized in Britain in 1926, but has since spread to the USA, where it was standardized in 1977. It is also found in the show pens of Australia and Europe. German breeders in particular made considerable effort to breed new colours.

Wales

BLUE SWEDISH

DRAKE

R enowned for its calm disposition, the Blue Swedish is an ideal orchard duck, as it loves to forage. It is thought to originate in northern Europe (writers have noted it since the mid-nineteenth century) and is distinctive for being a 'blue' duck. This colour proves a constant challenge for breeders to perfect, and was widely believed to make it hardy and more difficult for predators to track down.

Features

For both sexes, the body plumage should be a uniform shade of slate-blue, strongly laced with a darker shade of blue, apart from a white teardrop-shaped 'bib'. The drake's head has a greenish lustre, while the duck's is dark blue. The Blue Swedish has a full breast and a round, plump body.

Uses

Despite this duck's striking colour and its value on the show bench, the dinner table was its original place. It is also a reasonable layer of 120-plus eggs a year. Ducks are good foragers and good mothers, rearing strong, healthy ducklings. These factors made it an attractive breed for smallholders in the nineteenth century.

Related Breeds

The Blue Swedish originates from a similar area to the Pomeranian (Pommern) and they are sometimes mistaken for each other, although the Blue Swedish is larger.

Size

Drake .... 3.6 kg (8 lb)

Duck .... 3.2 kg (7 lb)

Origin and Distribution

This breed is believed to originate in parts of northern Europe controlled by Sweden in the mid-nineteenth century. It was developed on the Baltic shores of Germany and Poland, and reached the USA in 1884. It was standardized in Britain in 1982.

Sweden

INDIAN RUNNER
TROUT DRAKE

In Australia the INDIAN RUNNER was once described as the 'Leghorn of Duckdom' – the Leghorn being a high-laying hen. This description is not without merit, as up to 300 eggs per year have been recorded by some individuals. This bird revolutionized breeding programmes in the early twentieth century, lending its superior egg-laying skills to other duck breeds.

Features

The long, slim body is carried at an angle of 50–80 degrees when on the move – which the Indian Runner does at some speed! Typically a duck measures 60–70 cm (24–28 in) from tip of bill to tip of the middle toe. Completing its racy appearance is tight plumage, with the wings (which no longer fly) being carried tight to the body.

Use

This stunning duck is a popular choice with breeders for its variation of colours and is very much at home in the show pen. Yet when it first came to Britain it was its egg production that impressed duck-keepers. It likes to forage and can clear away slugs and snails between crops.

Related Breeds

The Bali, an equally historic breed, is a close relative of the Indian Runner, which has had a recognizable influence on the Abacot Ranger, Khaki Campbell, Orpington and Welsh Harlequin.

Size

Drake .... 1.6–2.3 kg (3½–5 lb)

Duck .... 1.4–2 kg (3–4½ lb)

Origin and Distribution

The Indian Runner is an ancient breed in Malaya, where it was first seen by British travellers. It was exhibited in Dumfries in 1876 and soon went worldwide, with enthusiasts in the USA, Australia and Europe.

Malaya

ROUEN CLAIR
DRAKE

Once thought to be more of a utility duck than the similar Rouen, the ROUEN CLAIR has an unusually long body, at around 90 cm (35 in) from bill to tail. It is an impressively large and colourful breed that excels as an exhibition duck. Breeders strive to produce a bird with the breeds' exacting colours.

Features

The long body (although wide) is carried 10–20 degrees above the horizontal, giving this breed an appearance of elegance, despite its impressive size. Like the Rouen, the Rouen Clair has Mallard colouring, but is lighter, although it retains the vividness and noticeable iridescent blue-tipped markings on the wing. The plumage is tight and smooth. The strong, short legs are a dull yellow-orange.

Use

The Rouen Clair was an archetypal farmyard duck, further developed in 1910–20 with birds from the Picardy area of France. The aim was to breed for plumage colour and size, and the result was a beautiful and eye-catching duck for exhibition, but also a useful commercial duck of the time, with a big, meaty carcass and good egg-laying ability.

Related Breeds

The Rouen is related to the Rouen Clair.

Size

Drake .... 3.4–4.1 kg (7½–9 lb)

Duck .... 2.9–3.4 kg (6½–7½ lb)

Origin and Distribution

Developed in France from the traditional Mallard-type duck of the area, the Rouen Clair was standardized in France in 1923. It is particularly associated with the Picardy areas but was exhibited in the Parisian shows. It was standardized in Britain in 1982 but appears to be less common worldwide than the related Rouen.

France

CRESTED

WHITE DRAKE

Popular because of its attractive headgear, the CRESTED is also a respectable egg-layer and a hardy outdoor type, being both active and alert. This breed's origins are unclear, but it was painted by Dutch artists in the seventeenth century and became very popular during the late twentieth century. In some countries it is known as a Tufta – a term that describes the appearance of the crest on the head.

Features

The Crested carries itself reasonably upright, but the real attraction is the crest, which should be well balanced and even, and firmly attached to the centre of the crown; the feathers grow from a globule of fatty tissue. The Crested is allowed to exhibit all colours. The Crested White (shown here) has blue eyes with an orange-yellow bill, legs and feet, setting off the pure-white plumage.

Use

Ducks with crests are difficult to breed for genetic reasons. The Crested is an ideal show bird, but is a challenge to breed and requires special care to keep the crest in good order and prevent the crest feathers being harmed by other ducks or spiky shrubs.

Related Breeds

The Crested Miniature was developed as the Bantam counterpart to the Crested. The Crested is also related to another crested duck, the Bali.

Size

Drake .... 3.2 kg (7 lb)

Duck .... 2.7 kg (6 lb)

Origin and Distribution

The breed's origins are uncertain, but it is thought to have come from Asia to Holland via the Dutch East India Company. Certainly this breed was seen in Europe in the early twentieth century and was standardized in Britain in 1910 and in the USA in 1874.

Holland

SAXONY

DRAKE

Bred by Albert Franz in East Germany in the 1930s, the development of the SAXONY was interrupted by the Second World War; the aim was to reduce the maturing time of the Rouen and improve the laying abilities – both of which goals were subsequently achieved when the post-war breeding programmes resumed.

Features

The Saxony's body is large and round, with a full breast. The drake (shown here) has a blue-grey head with a white neck ring about 5 mm (¼ in) wide, below which the breast and shoulders are a rich rusty-red; the body is oatmeal, the rump and back are blue-grey. The duck is an apricot-buff with an attractive white eye stripe. The colour markings are particularly important in the Standard, carrying nearly one-third of the 100 marks awarded.

Use

The Saxony is a useful egg-layer and provides a good meaty carcass. Its gentle personality, meaning it is pleasant to handle, and beautiful colours make it a desirable exhibition duck, but this non-flyer does require exercise in the form of a foraging area so that it does not get too plump.

Related Breeds

The Saxony was developed from Rouen, German Pekin and Blue Pomeranian ducks.

Size

Drake .... 3.6 kg (8 lb)

Duck .... 3.2 kg (7 lb)

Origin and Distribution

Bred in the 1930s in East Germany, the Saxony was recognized there in 1957 and in West Germany in 1958. It was standardized in Britain in 1982 and was admitted to the American *Standards of Perfection* in 2000. It is also found in Australia.

East Germany

MINIATURE SILVER APPLEYARD
DRAKE

Bred by Tom Bartlett in Britain some 30 years after Reginald Appleyard developed the original larger Silver Appleyard breed, the striking MINIATURE SILVER APPLEYARD was always destined for the show bench. At just one-third of the size of the original, it retains all the colour characteristics in a delightfully compact form, and also exemplifies the vigour and hardiness of the earlier utility breed.

Features

Although the emphasis is on colour, this breed must still show a compact, well-rounded body and carry itself slightly erect. In the drake (shown here) the head and neck are black overlaid with a green lustre, and a white ring must encircle the neck; deep claret covers the shoulders and back, while the breast is claret underlaid with white. The iridescent blue speculum or patch stands out against the grey and white wings.

Use

As the large Silver Appleyard was bred for meat and eggs, the Miniature has retained these characteristics. Initially standardized in 1997, this duck burst onto the show scene at the first British Waterfowl Association's Championship Waterfowl Exhibition.

Related Breeds

The large Silver Appleyard was used to create this miniature breed but the other breeds used are unknown.

Size

Drake .... 1.36 kg (3 lb)

Duck .... 1.19 kg (2½ lb)

Origin and Distribution

The 1980s saw the development of this breed by Tom Bartlett in Gloucestershire, England. It was first pictured in the poultry journal *Fancy Fowl* in 1986, next to its full-sized counterpart, and caused a stir. It has since spread to the USA and Australia where it is a valued show bird.

England

PEKIN

DUCK

K nown as the 'Penguin' duck due to its upright carriage, the PEKIN transformed the development of commercial table ducks when it was used in breeding. When the Pekin was imported to Britain in the late nineteenth century, its plumage was spoken of as having a yellowish hue, but deep cream or cream is now desirable in the show pen.

Features

A stately duck, whose upright carriage and impressive size account for almost half the total marks awarded, the Pekin has strong, stout legs set well back on the body. The plumage is almost fluffy and gives the impression of being plentiful. The Pekin has a bright-orange bill, and feet to match, and the eyes are a dark lead-blue, set high above full cheeks.

Use

The Pekin's success in the show pen today is secondary to its impressive record as a quick-maturing, high-yielding meat bird. When introduced to America, this breed quickly displaced the Cayuga as the leading table bird; it did the same to the Aylesbury in England. Pekins also lay a respectable number of eggs and they can make good mothers.

Related Breeds

The Pekin has no related breeds. It has, however, been used prolifically in cross-breeding programmes and has revolutionized the commercial table bird.

Size

Drake .... 4.1 kg (9 lb)

Duck .... 3.6 kg (8 lb)

Origin and Distribution

Originating in China around 2500BC, this duck is now found worldwide, both as a pure breed and as a cross. The Pekin is prized as an exhibition bird and is standardized in Britain, Europe, the USA and Australia.

China

INDIAN RUNNER

CHOCOLATE DUCK

Valued initially for their egg production, INDIAN RUNNERS were later bred for their carriage, and a number of different colours – such as this Chocolate Runner – were developed by enthusiasts. During the 1920s the ideal shape was considered to resemble the classic 'hock bottle'. It is the upright stance and the long, elegant neck that catch the eye, but this breed is also a fast mover and will range over a wide area.

Features

The Indian Runner has a long body, but its neck should not be less than one-third of its total length. The legs are set well back to give the upright stance. The plumage is tight and smooth, with the wings set close to the body, adding to the racy look of this breed. The Chocolate Runner (shown here) is one of a wide range of colours and was standardized in 1930.

Use

Mainly kept for its eye-catching stance and highly sought-after in the show pens, the Indian Runner was first valued for the impressively high number of eggs that it lays. When first imported into Britain it revolutionized attitudes towards egg-laying ducks.

Related Breeds

The Bali is a relation, and the Indian Runner lent its genes to utility ducks of the early twentieth century: the Khaki Campbell, Abacot Ranger, Orpington and Welsh Harlequin.

Size

Drake .... 1.6–2.3 kg (3½–5 lb)

Duck .... 1.4–2 kg (3–4½ lb)

Origin and Distribution

Originally found in Malaya, this breed was brought via trading routes to Britain, where it became popular as an egg-layer and exhibition duck and was standardized in 1901. It is well known in Europe, the USA and Australia.

Malaya

MINIATURE SILVER APPLEYARD

DUCK

A replica of the large Silver Appleyard duck bred by Reginald Appleyard, the MINIATURE SILVER APPLEYARD was bred by another enthusiast in Gloucestershire in the 1980s and is one of only two miniature duck breeds. Although the original Silver Appleyard was bred for meat and eggs, it is a devastatingly attractive duck, particularly in its miniature form.

Features

The Miniature is roughly one-third of the size of the large Silver Appleyard, but shares all the other characteristics, being compact and carrying itself slightly erect. The striking colour gets almost one-third of the overall marks. The female (shown here) has a range of delicate colours, from her fawn-flecked breast to the top of her silver-white neck and face and contrasting blue wing tips.

Use

This duck was specifically bred as a miniature version of the iconic Silver Appleyard and as a show bird. Its diminutive stature makes it delightful to handle, and it is an easy breeder. It retains many of the original utility characteristics of the Silver Appleyard, producing a good carcass and delicious eggs.

Related Breeds

The Miniature Silver Appleyard derives from its larger counterpart, the Silver Appleyard, and other unknown breeds.

Size

Drake .... 1.36 kg (3 lb)

Duck .... 1.19 kg (2½ lb)

Origin and Distribution

The Miniature Silver Appleyard was bred in Gloucestershire, England, in the 1980s by Tom Bartlett, and was standardized in 1997. For a breed that has only fairly recently come into existence, it has had great impact on the showing world. The Miniature is also found in Australia and the USA.

England

MINIATURE CRESTED

COLOURED DRAKE

An active bird that enjoys ranging, the diminutive MINIATURE CRESTED is distinguished by its pompom crest. It is a fairly recent introduction, having been bred in Yorkshire in the late 1980s, with the aim of producing a miniature variety of the eye-catching larger Crested duck. Breeders strive to produce a perfect crest, which is a continual challenge.

Features

The crest is all-important, and is awarded almost one-third of the marks. It is positioned on the crown of the head and must be well balanced, even and globular – a topknot, not straggly or flat. It is a small mass of fatty tissue from which feathers grow, and must not sit over the eyes. The Miniature Crested is allowed to exhibit all colours, but symmetry of markings is important.

Use

The Miniature Crested was developed solely as an ornamental exhibition bird. It takes considerable preparation to show off the crest at its best, and it must be kept clean and protected from anything that might cause damage. These miniatures also lay a respectable number of small but delicious eggs each year.

Related Breeds

The Crested and Call were used in the development and breeding of the Miniature Crested.

Size

Drake .... 1.1 kg (2½ lb)

Duck .... 0.9 kg (2 lb)

Origin and Distribution

The Miniature Crested was bred in Yorkshire, England, during the late 1980s and standardized in 1997. It is now found through-out Europe where keen breeders ensure that it is seen frequently on the show benches.

England

HOOK BILL

DRAKE

An ancient breed with a unique curved bill, the HOOK BILL is associated with the canals of Holland, where it was widely kept for eggs in the eighteenth century. It was almost self-sufficient, using its ability to fly and forage in order to feed itself. Charles Darwin described Hook Bills in his books, and is believed to have kept them.

Features

The upper neck, head and bill are strongly curved downwards, with the eyes set high in the head. The bill is awarded nearly one-third of the total marks for its Standard, and must not be short or straight. Hook Bills are round-breasted, with a fully developed underbody and a long, slender back. The three recognized colours are dusky mallard, white-bibbed dusky mallard (shown here) and white.

Use

The Hook Bill is now much valued as an ornamental exhibition bird, but was originally an almost maintenance-free bird for river dwellers. An average layer and useful table bird, the Hook Bill is also a good mother. Its curved bill distinguished it as a domestic breed, so it was not targeted by hunters.

Related Breeds

The Hook Bill is a unique breed and has no relations, except for its ancestor, the Mallard.

Size

Drake .... 2–2.25 kg (4½–5 lb)

Duck .... 1.6–2 kg (3½–4½ lb)

Origin and Distribution

The origins of this duck are obscure, but it is thought to have come from Asia to Holland via the Dutch trading routes. It is now found in Britain, Europe and America. It's called the Dutch Hook Bill in the USA and is in the 'Study' category for rare livestock breeds, making it unique.

Holland

INDIAN RUNNER

FAWN DRAKE

Its long body and its upright stance makes the INDIAN RUNNER instantly recognizable, in whichever of the many colours it is seen. The Fawn (shown here) is one of the most long established, and was first exhibited at a class for Fawns at Dumfries in 1876. The Indian Runner was the breed that introduced the concept of a high-laying duck – with up to 300 eggs per year being recorded by some individuals.

Features

The body is described in the Standards as 'slim, elongated and rounded'. The Indian Runner is a very active bird, with its well set-back legs enabling all-day foraging and quite high speeds. Many colours have been developed, from the original whole Fawn to today's exciting-sounding Apricot Dusky.

Use

The Indian Runner's impressive egg-laying record had a huge influence on other breeds being developed in the early twentieth century. Today, it is a natural for the show pen, and is also useful in a horticultural setting, where controlled foraging can help to clear the ground of slugs and snails in a natural way.

Related Breeds

The Bali and the Indian Runner have a related history, and Indian Runner crosses were used to develop utility breeds such as the Abacot Ranger, Orpington, Khaki Campbell and Welsh Harlequin.

Size

Drake .... 1.6–2.3 kg (3½–5 lb)

Duck .... 1.4–2 kg (3–4½ lb)

Origin and Distribution

The Indian Runner was imported from Malaya into Britain in the 1830s, and was finally standardized in 1901 in Fawn, White and Pied. It is also found in the USA, Australia and Europe.

Malaya

BLACK EAST INDIAN

DRAKE

The Black East Indian is generally thought – despite its name – to have originated in the USA around the nineteenth century. It is believed to have been imported to Britain in the mid-1800s by the Earl of Derby; it was first standardized in Britain in 1865. A good layer, its first eggs often appear to be covered in a sooty type of deposit, but eventually become a dull white.

Features

It is the plumage of this compact duck that is its most striking feature. Although black is the predominant colour, an intense beetle-green sheen covers much of the plumage and catches the eye. The strong wings are carried high against the close, glossy feathers. This breed has a black bill and black legs and feet.

Use

The Black East Indian is an impressive exhibition bird and is prized as an ornamental. This breed likes to be active, so one needs to bear that in mind when managing it. The better the bird's condition, the more striking the plumage – which is a vital part of an exhibition duck.

Related Breeds

The Black East Indian has similar colour characteristics to the Cayuga and may have the same ancestor – a close relative of the Mallard, the American black duck.

Size

Drake .... 0.9 kg (2 lb)

Duck .... 0.7–0.8 kg (1½–1¾ lb)

Origin and Distribution

The USA is the most likely country of origin, although the Black East Indian was also known in South America and the East Indies. It is standardized in Britain and America, and can be seen in the Australian and European show pen.

USA

SILVER BANTAM

DUCK

It is believed that Reginald Appleyard (the breeder of the Silver Appleyard) developed the SILVER BANTAM with designs for a Silver Appleyard Bantam. But the name of his breed was changed to Silver Bantam when the Silver Appleyard Miniature was standardized in 1997. In appearance this bird is closer to the Abacot Ranger than the Silver Appleyard.

Features

This is a compact duck with a slightly erect carriage. The duck (shown here) has a fawn head and neck grained with dark brown, divided from the white breast; the primary feathers are silvery white (as are the drake's), with a bluish-green-tipped speculum; breast and flanks are streaked with light brown; the underbody is creamy-white. The drake has a black head with a green lustre to the white neck ring and a claret breast.

Use

The Silver Bantam is an attractive and unusual duck in the show pen, although it is quite difficult to breed the correct colour and markings. It is a fairly good layer of delicious small eggs and naturally docile, making it ideal for pen-taming.

Related Breeds

The Silver Bantam is thought to be the small version of the Silver Appleyard large duck, but is more likely a cross between a White Call and a Khaki Campbell.

Size

Drake .... 0.9 kg (2 lb)

Duck .... 0.8 kg (1¾ lb)

Origin and Distribution

The Silver Bantam was bred in Suffolk, England, by Reginald Appleyard and first appeared in the Standards in 1982 as the Silver Appleyard Bantam – changed in 1997 to the Silver Bantam. It is found in Europe, but is not widespread elsewhere.

England

MUSCOVY

BLACK & WHITE DRAKE

In 1908 the *New Zealand Poultry Journal* asserted that the Muscovy was a 'wild and terrible bird to fly'. It is, in fact, an exceptionally good flyer, and a devoted mother, with hens sitting on their eggs for 35 days rather than the 28 of other ducks. Unlike other domestic ducks with the Mallard as a common ancestor, the Muscovy is descended from a perching duck from Central and South America.

Features

If you alarm the Muscovy, the small crest of feathers on its head will rise. The striking red protuberances on the face and base of the bill are known as caruncles. The wings are very strong and long, reflecting its superb flying ability. Strong, short legs support the long, powerful body, and the feet show pronounced toenails. The many colour variations include black, blue, chocolate, lavender and white, plus magpie (a solid colour and white, as shown here).

Use

The Muscovy spread along trade routes, being highly adaptable, with large white eggs and good meat qualities. A good mother and forager, this breed is hardy to keep. It was standardized in 1954, with new colours being developed from the original, mainly black bird.

Related Breeds

The Muscovy is a unique breed, for it is the only domestic duck that does not have the Mallard as a common ancestor.

Size

Drake .... 4.5–6.3 kg (10–14 lb)

Duck .... 2.3–3.2 kg (5–7 lb)

Origin and Distribution

Originating in South and Central America, the Muscovy is believed to have been domesticated prior to Columbus's appearance there in 1492. It is now found throughout the world and is exhibited in Europe, the USA and Australia.

South &
Central America

SILVER APPLEYARD
DUCK

When Reginald Appleyard bred the SILVER APPLEYARD in Suffolk during the 1940s, he managed to produce not only a prolific egg-laying duck that was good for the table, but also a duck of such great beauty that it is now prized as an exhibition bird. It is classified as a Heavy duck, although its appearance is rather active, underlining this breed's good foraging ability.

Features

This bird has striking colouring. The duck (shown here) has a silver-white head with fawn flecked with brown-grey down the neck, continuing over the back and rump; the breast and underbody are creamy-white. The drake has a black-lustred green head and neck with a white ring, below which the breast shows claret fading to silver. The plumage is close and smooth, and the wings are held tight to the body.

Use

Mr Appleyard produced a top-class utility bird with white skin for the table, impressive laying ability, quick maturation and good foraging skills. The Silver Appleyard was finally standardized in 1982 and makes a great exhibition bird.

Related Breeds

The Silver Appleyard is thought to include Rouen Clair blood and some Pekin, but Mr Appleyard did not share his method of breeding the bird. The Miniature Silver Appleyard was developed as a Bantam breed.

Size

Drake .... 3.6–4.1 kg (8–9 lb)

Duck .... 3.2–3.6 kg (7–8 lb)

Origin and Distribution

The breed was developed in Suffolk, England, and reached the USA in 1964. Breeder Tom Bartlett re-awoke interest in it, using a painting of the bird by poultry artist E. G. Wippell as a standard for his miniature breed. It is also found in Europe and Australia.

England

CAYUGA

DRAKE

The beetle-green sheen of its plumage characterizes the CAYUGA, which is said to have been bred from a pair of wild black ducks, trapped by a miller on his pond in New York in the early 1800s. It takes its name from the Native American Cayuga people. It was included in the American Poultry Association's *Standard of Perfection* in 1874, and then standardized in Britain in 1901.

Features

Both sexes are black, and it is the beetle-green lustre of the Cayuga's plumage that means colour is awarded the highest number of points in the Breed Standard. It must appear smooth-feathered, tight and glossy. The head should be large, with full, bold eyes, and the neck graceful, while the body is long, broad and deep. The black bill and legs accentuate this stunning bird.

Use

This duck produces dark-coloured meat, yet it was the principal meat-duck in the USA until the introduction of the Pekin there in 1873. However, it was soon being kept for show as well. Breeders revelled in producing the perfect colour specimen. Although not a great egg-layer, the first eggs have a sooty layer overlying the white shell.

Related Breeds

The Black East Indian may share the same American wild black-duck ancestor of the Cayuga.

Size

Drake .... 3.6 kg (8 lb)

Duck .... 3.2 kg (7 lb)

Origin and Distribution

Cayugas were bred on Lake Cayuga in New York State, and had reached Britain by 1901. Today this breed is also found throughout Europe and in Australia. It is particularly valued for its impressive plumage at waterfowl exhibitions.

New York State

CAMPBELL
KHAKI DUCK

The Khaki CAMPBELL (shown here) was bred in 1901 as a utility duck that laid a high number of eggs, but also had a carcass suitable for the dinner table. It was developed to be an active forager and not go broody, as sitting and rearing ducklings would limit the number of eggs produced. It soon became the most widely kept duck for egg production in both small farms and commercial situations.

Features

The carriage of the Campbell is semi-upright. The Khaki was patriotically named not only for its body colour, but also to remember the soldiers fighting in the Boer Wars. Khaki in colour, the drake has a green-bronze head and neck, while the duck is an even shade of warm khaki, which is slightly darker around the head and neck.

Use

The Khaki Campbell is an outstanding egg-layer, regularly topping laying trials during and post-war. Despite Mrs Campbell's reluctance to develop a standard, due to her fear that the utility characteristics would be lost, these days it is a regular at shows.

Related Breeds

The original Khaki Campbell is believed to have been a Rouen and Indian Runner cross, but may also have included some wild-duck blood. The White Campbell, Welsh Harlequin and Abacot Ranger are variants on this breed.

Size

Drake .... 2.3–2.5 kg (5–5½ lb)

Duck .... 2–2.3 kg (4½–5 lb)

Origin and Distribution

The Campbell breed originated in Mrs Campbell's orchard in Gloucestershire, England, but is now found throughout the duck-showing world.

England

CALL

YELLOW BELLY DUCK

The cute CALL is a diminutive breed, classified as a Bantam duck. Having been first imported to Britain in the mid-nineteenth century as a working duck, it soon made its way onto the show scene and was standardized in Britain in 1865. The breed enjoyed a resurgence of popularity during the 1970s, following further imports from Holland.

Features

With its compact body, round head, large eyes, full cheeks and high crown, the Call is instantly appealing. The Yellow Belly (shown here) shows a range of entrancing colours, but particularly eye-catching in the female is the pinkish-buff breast topping a light buff underbody. The male and female resemble the wild Mallard colouring 'above the water line', but below it show a dominant pale pinkish-buff.

Use

A very vocal duck, the Call was originally a working bird, used to lure wild ducks for trapping. Today it is highly popular on the show scene and comes in an impressive range of colours. Easy to tame and manage and brimming with personality, it also makes a popular pet.

Related Breeds

Some crossing with Call ducks was used in developing the Miniature Crested.

Size

Drake .... 0.6–0.7 kg (1¼–1½ lb)

Duck .... 0.5–0.6 kg (1–1¼ lb)

Origin and Distribution

The Call is now widely distributed throughout the world, although it is known for its Dutch origins in the seventeenth century. It is thought that it probably came to Holland from Asia via well-established trading routes.

Holland

BALI

COLOURED DRAKE

Distinctive for the crest on its head and upright stance, the Bali is still part of life in Bali, where it is used to clear pests from rice fields. It does not fly, but flocks together, making it easy to move around crops. Although ancient stone carvings indicate its very long history, it was only introduced to the UK in 1925 and finally standardized in 1930.

Features

The Breed Standard places most importance on the Bali's crest: 25 points are applicable to the head, bill and neck, and it should be a single, globular crest to the rear of the head. The strong legs set to the rear of the bird create its upright carriage. Any colour is permitted, but symmetrical markings are desirable.

Use

For generations this duck has been used in Bali to eat the pests in the rice fields; it is led into the fields by day and then back to secure housing at night. As recent Bali ducks have been re-created using Indian Runner crosses, it is also a respectable layer. It is an impressive exhibitor due to its upright stance, elegant head and all-important crest.

Related Breeds

The Indian Runner is a close relation, historically and more recently, when Indian Runner blood was used to re-create the breed.

Size

Drake .... 2.3 kg (5 lb)

Duck .... 1.8 kg (4 lb)

Origin and Distribution

The Bali originates from the Indonesian island of Bali. Numbers fell in Britain after its importation in the 1920s, leading to a re-creation of the breed in the 1990s. The Bali is spreading to other countries, but is not standardized in all of them.

Bali

CALL
BLACK DUCK

Classified as a Bantam duck, the CALL is one of the smallest of the duck breeds. Its piercing and repeated cry is accurately captured by the Dutch name *Kwaker*, and it was this persistent call that led to Calls being used as decoy ducks by hunters in the mid-nineteenth century. Today it is a particularly popular breed both on the show scene and in the pet trade.

Features

The Call's compact, round body and horizontal carriage are valued in the Breed Standard, carrying more than one-third of the total marks. The Black Call (shown here) must be a uniform shade of black, except for the head and neck, which may show some lustrous green sheen. The bill is black, and although black legs are also preferred, some orange pigment is acceptable.

Use

The Call's loud, persistent quack was originally used to draw in wild ducks to the hunters, but it is now an ornamental duck widely used for showing. It is bred in an impressively wide range of colours, with more being developed. It makes a good guard duck, as it will quack loudly at any visitors – wanted or unwanted.

Related Breeds

Some crossing with Call ducks was used in developing the Miniature Crested.

Size

Drake .... 0.6–0.7 kg (1¼–1½ lb)

Duck .... 0.5–0.6 kg (1–1¼ lb)

Origin and Distribution

Believed to have arrived in Holland from Asia as part of the trading routes, the Call was recorded as a decoy duck in the Netherlands from the seventeenth century. Two colours were standardized in Britain in 1865, and today it is a popular breed throughout the world.

Holland

MINIATURE CRESTED

COLOURED DUCK

A designer duck, bred in the late 1980s with exhibition in mind, the fairytale MINIATURE CRESTED is still an active bird that enjoys ranging. Using Call ducks, breeders have developed an engaging and charming breed that sits naturally in the show pen and whose spectacular crest is a continual challenge for breeders to perfect.

Features

The globular crest, also known as a topknot or pompom, is positioned in the centre of the crown of the head. In appearance it should look dense, rather than loose, and must not cover the eyes. All colours are permitted in the Miniature Crested, but points are awarded for symmetry of markings. The carriage should be reasonably upright, with a long, broad (but small) body.

Use

The aim of breeding the Miniature Crested was to produce a smaller replica of the Crested duck, as an ornamental exhibition bird. Such ducks have to be kept away from anything that might damage their crest – and that includes mating – and must be kept in clean conditions to retain their topknot in tip-top condition. It's a useful egg layer.

Related Breeds

In the development of this miniature form of the Crested duck, breeders made use of the Call duck.

Size

Drake .... 1.1 kg (2½ lb)

Duck .... 0.9 kg (2 lb)

Origin and Distribution

Although the Miniature Crested is now found throughout Europe, it was originally bred in Yorkshire, England, in the late 1980s. It was standardized in Britain in 1997. Due to the crest being a 'lethal gene', this duck can be a challenge to breed.

England

INDIAN RUNNER

FAWN & WHITE DRAKE

The long-bodied INDIAN RUNNER becomes almost upright when on the alert – or when trained to 'pose' by its exhibitor. The slim neck must comprise at least one-third of the total length of the duck, from the tip of the skull to top of the tail, giving an elongated but elegant appearance. Yet the Indian Runner is also a useful duck, with an impressive egg-laying performance.

Features

The tight plumage and wings packed close to the body give the bird its slim line. To create the upright carriage, the legs – with their powerful thighs and flexible feet – are set well back on the body. A wide range of colours have been developed; Fawn and White (shown here) was standardized as a colour in 1901.

Use

It was the Indian Runner's superior egg-laying skills which had everyone talking in the early twentieth century. Today it is still kept for its eggs, as well as for showing, and as a 'gardener's friend', for its foraging ability helps to clear the land of pests. It can also be used to demonstrate sheepdog skills, for Indian Runners flock together and can be directed where to move.

Related Breeds

This breed is related to the equally ancient Bali. In the twentieth century duck breeders introduced Indian Runner blood into the Abacot Ranger, Orpington, Khaki Campbell and Welsh Harlequin.

Size

Drake .... 1.6–2.3 kg (3½–5 lb)

Duck .... 1.4–2 kg (3–4½ lb)

Origin and Distribution

The Indian Runner was documented in Malaya prior to being imported to Britain in the early nineteenth century. It is now well known in Europe, the USA and Australia.

Malaya

WELSH HARLEQUIN
LIGHT DRAKE

Group Captain Leslie Bonnet developed the hardy WELSH HARLEQUIN from Khaki Campbell 'sports' (pure breeds that do not resemble the normal breed) among others. He nearly lost them, however, in the 1960s when his breeding flock was almost wiped out in a fox attack. Luckily, other keepers had retained some of the original stock and the breed was saved and finally had the Standard accepted in 1987.

Features

The Welsh Harlequin's compact body is carried on well set-apart legs, and the tight, glossy plumage shows a range of beautiful colours. The bronze-green head of the drake (shown here) leads to a white neck ring and mahogany shoulders; the underbody is creamy-white. The duck is honey-fawn on the head and neck, with a fawn to cream body; the closely held wings are laced.

Use

The Welsh Harlequin is valued on the show bench, being a challenge to breeders to achieve the correct colour. However, it was developed as a utility duck and lays up to 200 eggs a year, with a good table carcass, despite being a Light breed.

Related Breeds

The Welsh Harlequin is closely related to the Khaki Campbell (which in turn has Indian Runner blood).

Size

Drake .... 2.3–2.5 kg (5–5½ lb)

Duck .... 2–2.3 kg (4–5 lb)

Origin and Distribution

Group Captain Leslie Bonnet began breeding the Welsh Harlequin in Hertfordshire, England, but moved to north Wales, where the breed was named. It was accepted into the American *Standards of Perfection* in 2001 and is found in Europe as well as Australia.

England

ROUEN

DUCK

As the name suggests, the ROUEN was first noticed in Normandy in France during the eighteenth century. Once considered a fine table bird, this breed is now kept mainly for exhibition, as it matures very slowly, taking up to 20 weeks to get its adult feathers. The Rouen was initially standardized in Britain in 1865, making it one of the first breeds to be recognized.

Features

The impressive size and shape of the Rouen first draw attention. The carriage is low to the ground; the body is long and broad, with a wide, deep breast. The colour is that of a very bright, oversized Mallard in both duck and drake, and carries a detailed colour Standard. The drake will be disqualified for *not* having a neck ring, and the duck for having anything approaching a white neck ring.

Use

Originally bred as a meat bird, producing a rather dark meat, the Rouen also lays a reasonable number of large eggs. Today the show ring is the principal place for this breathtaking duck, for which its gentle temperament and very striking physical characteristics make it ideal.

Related Breeds

The Rouen Clair is related to the Rouen.

Size

Drake .... 4.5–5.4 kg (10–12 lb)

Duck .... 4.1–5 kg (9–11 lb)

Origin and Distribution

First recorded in France in the 1700s, around the city of Rouen, this breed reached the USA as early as 1874, where it is now in the 'Watch' classification of the American Livestock Conservancy. The Rouen is found throughout Europe and in the show pens of Australia. It is especially popular in Britain, where it is an impressive show bird.

France

OVERBERG

DUCK

Bred selectively in Holland, the OVERBERG was designed to produce up to 200 eggs a year and at the same time to be a good bird for the table. Calm and therefore ideal for domestication, this breed remains an active forager. The Overberg is often seen in show pens in Britain, but has yet to be recognized in the Breed Standard.

Features

Likened by some to a bluish version of the Welsh Harlequin, the Overberg has a rounded, medium body, with strong legs and very sleek plumage. It moves in a slightly upright fashion and does not 'waddle'. The duck (shown here) is pale yellow across the breast and flanks, changing to a dark-cream belly. The drake has a pale lilac-blue head and neck, with a wide white ring around the neck; the breast and flanks are mahogany-brown with white lacing, and the speculum is pale lilac-blue.

Use

This active, alert breed has a pleasant temperament. The duck was selectively bred to be a good layer and produce a meaty carcass for the table, but is now making its way into show pens in Britain, thanks to enthusiasts.

Related Breeds

The Abacot Ranger, the Hook Bill and the Welsh Harlequin are all believed to be related to the Overberg through selective breeding.

Size

Drake .... 2.3–2.5 kg (5–5½ lb)

Duck .... 2–2.3 kg (4½–5 lb)

Origin and Distribution

Having initially been developed in Holland, the Overberg is now found at exhibitions in Britain, but has not as yet been standardized. Its distribution worldwide is therefore unclear.

Holland

CAMPBELL
WHITE DRAKE

The original CAMPBELLS were bred in Gloucestershire in 1901, with Khaki being the first recognized colour. This duck was bred to lay a very high number of eggs, but also to be fit for the table. The White Campbell (shown here) was produced for a market that preferred a white table bird and was standardized in 1954.

Features

As an active forager, the Campbell has an upright carriage with a high head and strong legs. The head should be elegant and alert, but the overall appearance is one of a purposeful, hardy duck. The eyes are grey-blue. The White's plumage should be tight and sleek, with the wings held tight to the body.

Use

The Campbell is known for its outstanding egg-laying abilities: 300-plus eggs a year were recorded from individual Khaki Campbells in laying trials between the wars. Yet the original aim of their creator, Mrs Campbell, was to produce roast duckling for her family. This breed is the perfect all-rounder, producing eggs and meat in a back-yard or commercial situation. On the show bench its stature and colour make it an interesting bird.

Related Breeds

The White Campbell, the Welsh Harlequin and the Abacot Ranger are all variants on this breed. The original Khaki Campbell (believed to be a Rouen and Indian Runner cross) may have included some wild-duck blood.

Size

Drake .... 2.3–2.5 kg (5–5½ lb)

Duck .... 2–2.3 kg (4½–5 lb)

Origin and Distribution

Mrs Campbell bred her original Campbells in Gloucestershire, England, although the breed is now widespread throughout the world due to its usefulness.

England

MUSCOVY
BLACK DUCK

Love it or hate it, the MUSCOVY is a breed that simply cannot be ignored. The only domestic duck breed to originate from a perching tree duck rather than from a Mallard, it is full of personality, with its fleshy red protuberances on the face, or caruncles. It carries its body low to the ground, but moves in a lively way and is a determined flyer.

Features

The striking face distinguishes this unique duck, which has large wings, short, powerful legs and a broad body. On the head a small crest of feathers will rise, if the bird is alarmed. The feet show toenails, typical of a perching duck. The Black Muscovy (shown here) must show dense black plumage with a metallic lustre. Other plain variations include blue, chocolate, lavender and white, along with some magpie colourings.

Use

Standardized in 1954, the Muscovy is increasingly seen in the show pen, but it was for its meat and eggs that this bird was domesticated for so long. It is adaptable and a good mother, a keen forager and a surprisingly good flyer, given its appearance.

Related Breeds

The Muscovy is the only domestic duck that does not have the Mallard as a common ancestor. It is therefore considered a unique breed.

Size

Drake .... 4.5–6.3 kg (10–14 lb)

Duck .... 2.3–3.2 kg (5–7 lb)

Origin and Distribution

Central and South America were the Muscovy's original home, where it was domesticated for more than 500 years. The breed has now spread worldwide and is shown in Europe, Australia and the USA.

South and Central America

INDIAN RUNNER

BLACK DRAKE

The almost perpendicular stance of this duck when startled or trained for the show pen, plus its distinctive bottle shape with the long, elegant neck, makes the INDIAN RUNNER visually exciting. It is also a highly productive bird, and it left its mark on several other breeds when its genes were introduced for their egg-laying capabilities.

Features

The long, slim body is carried upright when on the alert, but at 50–80 degrees on the move – the legs being set far back to facilitate this. The head is elegant, with the eyes set high up, and the neck must comprise at least one-third of the duck's total length. Typically a duck measures 60–70 cm (24–28 in). The range of colours includes black (shown here), on which the tight, smooth plumage shows a green sheen.

Use

An eye-catching duck in the show pen, the Indian Runner remains a prolific egg-layer. It is also a great foraging duck, seeking out invertebrates and even being used commercially for this purpose, and can be seen at sheepdog and duck displays, much to the delight of crowds, as it has a flocking habit.

Related Breeds

The Bali is an ancient relative, and the Indian Runner's superior egg-laying ability was used in the development of the Abacot Ranger, Orpington, Khaki Campbell and Welsh Harlequin. The Black Runner was developed using the Black East Indian.

Size

Drake .... 1.6–2.3 kg (3½–5 lb)

Duck .... 1.4–2 kg (3–4½ lb)

Origin and Distribution

The Indian Runner was found in Malaya and came via trade routes to Britain; the Dumfries show of 1876 had a class of Fawn Runners. The breed soon spread to the USA and Australia, and is popular throughout Europe.

Malaya

CALL

APRICOT DRAKE

With its large eyes and round face, the cute CALL is the quintessential 'bathtime' rubber duck. These appealing looks have made it a natural for the show pens, where its character and its range of colours make it popular with breeders – and with pet owners – around the globe. New and interesting colour variations of the Call continue to be bred.

Features

The type and size of this duck are important features: its body must be compact, broad and deep, and its head round, with full cheeks and a high crown bearing bright eyes. The Apricot drake (shown here) shows a range of colours in its glossy plumage, from the silver-grey head to the claret breast and apricot-brown stippling on its flanks and underbelly. The duck is predominantly apricot in a variety of shades.

Use

Originally used to hunt wild ducks, the Call has been an ornamental duck for most of the twentieth century. Its lively and curious personality means it exhibits to advantage in the show pen. It is also a popular pet, content with a small man-made pond and being good with children, if well handled.

Related Breeds

The Miniature Crested was developed using some crossing with Call ducks.

Size

Drake .... 0.6–0.7 kg (1¼–1½ lb)

Duck .... 0.5–0.6 kg (1–1¼ lb)

Origin and Distribution

The Call's earliest origins are thought to have been in Asia, but it was documented in Holland from at least the seventeenth century. Its use as a decoy duck was recorded in the mid-nineteenth century in Britain, and two colours were standardized in 1865. These days it is a popular ornamental breed worldwide.

Holland

CALL
WHITE DUCK

The most diminutive duck in size and yet the largest duck in voice, the CALL was originally used as a decoy duck to lure wildfowl towards hunters' guns and nets with its loud and repetitive quacking. First documented in Holland during the seventeenth century, it is now well established in Britain as an ornamental show bird.

Features

With its small but deeply compact body, topped by a round head and large eyes, the Call is often thought of as the archetypal bathtub duck. The White Call (shown here) was one of the first two colours standardized in Britain in 1865, and is still often regarded as the hallmark of the breed. The plumage must be pure white and the eyes leaden blue. The bright orange legs and bright orange-yellow bill emphasize the whiteness of the feathers.

Use

Despite its history as a working bird, helping to provide fresh meat from wild ducks, the Call has now settled into its role as an ornamental exhibition bird, with its confident and charming personality making that adjustment easy. It is also a remarkably popular breed in the pet trade.

Related Breeds

The Miniature Crested duck was developed using some crossing with Calls.

Size

Drake .... 0.6–0.7 kg (1¼–1½ lb)

Duck .... 0.5–0.6 kg (1–1¼ lb)

Origin and Distribution

Although it has been known in Holland since the seventeenth century, the Call is thought to have entered that country from Asia via the trading routes. Its popularity has grown in Britain since its introduction in the mid-1800s, and the breed has now spread throughout the world.

Holland

CAMPBELL

DARK DUCK

Campbells are famous for their laying ability and were one of the first (and are still the most successful) of the utility breeds, which were designed to be high egg-layers and yet produce a carcass fit for the table. The original Khaki CAMPBELL was developed in 1901 by Mrs Campbell at her Gloucestershire orchard; other colour variations were later bred by enthusiasts.

Features

The Campbell's head is carried high on a slightly upright body, with full, bold eyes set fairly high in the head. The plumage should be tight and sleek, with the wings held tight to the body. It is an elegant but workmanlike duck in appearance. The Dark Campbell (shown here) has finely stippled feathers in shades of brown throughout the whole body, and both sexes have darker-coloured head and necks.

Use

Although now popular in poultry shows, this duck is still kept for its egg-laying abilities and hardy, active manner. The Dark Campbell is unique in that male and female ducklings are different colours, enabling early sexing.

Related Breeds

The original Khaki Campbell is thought to have been a Rouen and Indian Runner cross, but may also have included some wild-duck blood. The White Campbell, Welsh Harlequin and Abacot Ranger are all variants on this breed.

Size

Drake .... 2.3–2.5 kg (5–5½ lb)

Duck .... 2–2.3 kg (4½–5 lb)

Origin and Distribution

The Campbell breed originates from Gloucestershire in England, although the Dark Campbell was bred in Devon. The breed spread worldwide, but is on the American Livestock Conservancy's 'Watch' list.

England

BALI

WHITE DRAKE

With its very upright carriage, the BALI, which was first seen 2,000 or more years ago on the Indonesian island, looks like an Indian Runner with a crest. In fact the modern British bird is not so far from this, for it was re-created using Indian Runners. There is also speculation that the original Bali duck may have been the ancestor of the Indian Runner.

Features

The size and set of the crest, coupled with the upright body set on strong legs made for running, create a striking duck. The plumage of the White Bali must be pure white, as well as tight and hard. The eyes are blue, which makes this bird particularly captivating, and the bright-orange legs and orange-yellow bill set off the whiteness of the feathers.

Use

In Bali, this breed is still used to clear pests in rice fields; in Britain, these active foragers will eagerly snap up pests in the garden. Producing Bali ducks with a perfect crest for exhibition is a tough task: it is imperative that the crest is neat, tidy and well placed on an elegant head, and not overwhelming the duck.

Related Breeds

The Indian Runner is closely related to the Bali, both historically and in more recent times when it was used to re-create the breed with great success.

Size

Drake .... 2.3 kg (5 lb)

Duck .... 1.8 kg (4 lb)

Origin and Distribution

The Bali is native to the Indonesian island of Bali, east of Java. It was imported to Britain in the 1920s and has now reached much of Europe. In its native land the Bali can still be seen in rice fields.

Bali

REPORTAGE

Collective nouns for ducks include a *paddling* or *plump*, a *flock*, *flight* or *flush*. It's time to look behind the scenes as our *bevy* of beautiful birds prepare and PREEN for their big day at the show. The odd perfectly groomed feather may *fly* as we pull back the curtain and watch them at work.

Scottish National
Poultry Show, UK

National Poultry Show, UK

Domestic Waterfowl Club Show, UK

show kit:
✓ soapy water
✓ Brush
✓ Towel
✓ Oil

'The name's Pond,
James Pond!'

Everything looks in
order. It's show time!

That should fit the bill nicely.

Washed, groomed, oiled ... no flies on this one.

To do list:
√ Judge
√ Assess
√ Scrutinize
(I love my job)

Gently now...
I hate this bit.

Don't ruffle my feathers
or I may fly off the handle.

On a wing ...

... and a prayer ...

... we are going for Best in Show this year.

Possible winner. Prepare the rosette.

LIGHT BREED DUCK

PEN NO.

Championship Row is Sponsored BY RBST

4435

Note to Lady Gaga:
We have the best headgear
in town.

Checklist:
✓ Freshness
✓ Appearance
✓ Bloom

First Prize
THE POULTRY CL...
NATIONAL CHAMPIONSHIP...
CLASS 1179
PEN No. 663
www.fancyfowl.com

Thanks very much.

It's all in the shape,
symmetry ...

... and shell texture.

Note to all entrants next year: Keep up the prize-winning standards. No winging it!

Check out my profile!

We're all winners!

I would love to chat more but I have a prize to win.

LIGHT BREED DUCKS

SMALL HOLDER RANGE

AVY BREED DUCKS

SMALL HOLDER RANGE

This one is a real winner!

Note to self:
Check out webbedsite
www.duckoftheyear.com

Yes, I did clean my bill last night.

This is my best side.

Hold on to your hats, ladies. We're on the move.

I love every aspect of my job ...

...STIC WATERFOWL CLUB
...EN CHAMPIONSHIP SHOW
First Prize

... but this is the best bit.
RESULT!

It is not a matter of luck,
To have a champion duck,
Hours of breeding and care,
Will help to get you there,
So to all those seeking the cup,
We ducks say 'Bottoms up!'

Up close and personal.

Hurrah! We did it!

Back in the pen, hen.

Checklist
(for judge and entrants)
√ Health
√ Cleanliness
√ Brightness

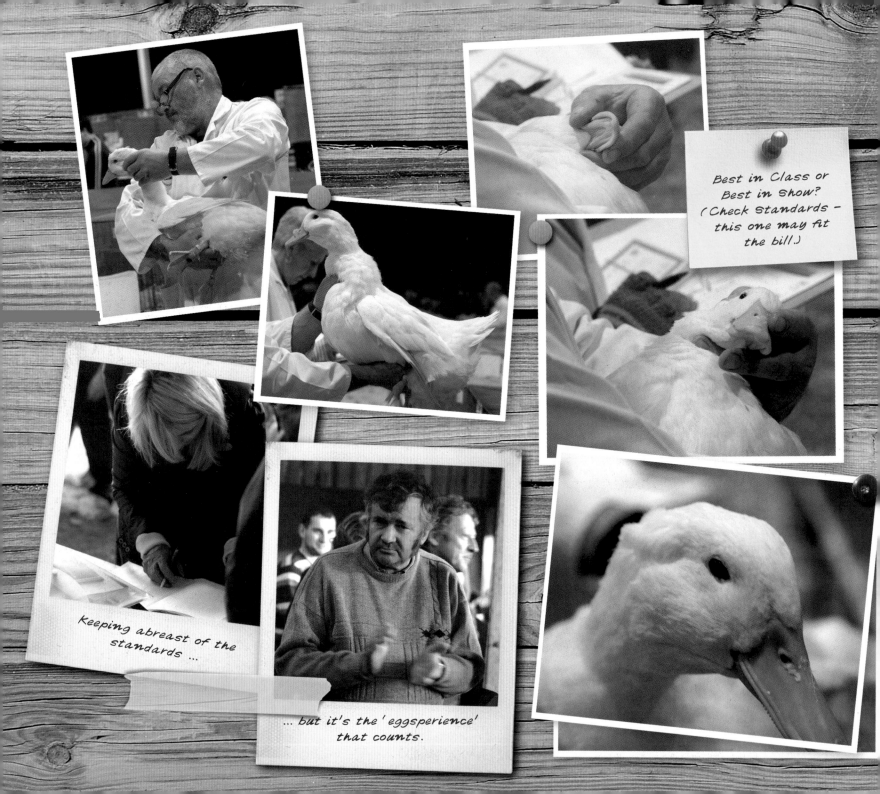

Best in Class or Best in Show? (Check standards – this one may fit the bill.)

Keeping abreast of the standards ...

... but it's the 'eggsperience' that counts.

Three 'Ps' for the Cups and Ducks:
Prepare,
Polish,
Present

I want one of those...

THE POULTRY CLUB
NATIONAL CHAMPIONSHIP
SHOW 2010

CHAMPION
HEAVY BREED DUCK

PEN NO......................

GLOSSARY

AOC Any Other Colour (show classification)

AOV Any Other Variety (show classification)

Auto-sexing male and female are different colours as ducklings, enabling them to be easily sexed

Bantam a small variety of duck: either a miniature variety of a larger breed or a small distinct breed

Bill the mouthparts of the bird, consisting of the upper and lower mandibles (jaws)

Breast the front of the bird's body

Breed club the governing body of each breed, which develops the 'Standards'; not all breeds have their own club, for they may come under the umbrella of a club that covers several breeds

Breed Standard *see* Standard

Broodiness the instinct of a duck to sit on eggs

Carriage the angle of the body to the ground

Caruncle a fleshy protuberance on the face of Muscovy ducks; these are more pronounced in the drakes

Collar a band of colour around the neck, usually white or silver

Coverts small feathers on the wing and tail that surround the bases of the larger feathers

Crest tufted feathers, ideally positioned on the centre of the head

Cross-breeding the breeding of two separate breeds together – often the starting process of forming new breeds or colours

Decoy duck a vocal duck whose noise attracts wild ducks into lakes, for hunters to kill

Drake a male duck

Duck a generic term for the species, but also used to describe a female duck

Duckling a term for a duck from hatching to the time when feathers have replaced the down

Fancier a competitor in the show-poultry world (which is sometimes described as 'The Fancy')

Flank the part of the body lying between the ribs and hips

Flight the large feather of the wings, connected by tissue to the bone; there are wing flights, primary, secondary and tertial flights, as well as tail flights, although people frequently use the term to describe only the primaries

Foraging the ability to search for invertebrates and vegetable matter when let out on range

Heavy a large duck usually developed for the table; this group now contains some of the most impressive show birds

Lacing a feather edged by a darker stripe

Lustre a sheen over the plumage

Light a duck that tends to be a good egg-layer; some of this group also provide a reasonable carcass

Moult the shedding of feathers and their replacement by new ones

Pen training the taming and handling of a duck to acclimatize it to the show environment

Pin feathers newly emerging feathers after a moult

Neck ring a collar that encircles the neck, usually in white or silver

Pied white and another colour

Preening lubricating feathers using the preening gland at the base of the rump, which needs to be activated by water

Primaries the 10 main flight feathers on a wing

Rump the lower back above the tail

Scale of Points the exhibition duck is judged out of 100 points, and breeds have different point weightings for colour, body shape, head and neck

Secondaries the inner flight feathers

Sex curls curls on a drake's tail that denote maleness

Speculum a patch, often distinctively coloured, on the secondary feathers of the wing

Sport an example of a pure breed that does not resemble the normal breed – for example, a light-coloured duck in a breed that is normally dark

Standard criteria agreed by breed clubs for a particular breed – the ideal duck, according to each country's specification

Tertiaries the feathers attached to the wing bone closest to the body and overlying the secondaries

Trio a male and two females

Table birds ducks that are bred for meat

Underbelly/underbody the area below the wings and along the belly of the duck

Utility birds ducks bred for meat and for their egg-laying ability

Waterfowl birds that naturally spend much time on water

Wildfowl breeds that exist in the wild, usually kept in collections and not used for egg-laying or meat; they are sometimes known as ornamentals

SHOWS

BRITAIN
Poultry shows that include waterfowl classes are held all year round, but in Britain the big championship shows are held in the autumn months after the breeding season.

October: Shropshire and Mid-Wales Waterfowl Exhibition; Welsh Federation of Poultry Clubs

November: British Waterfowl Association National Championship Show; Devon and Cornwall Waterfowl Show; Domestic Waterfowl Club Championship Show; Poultry Club of Great Britain National Championship Show

December: National Federation of Poultry Clubs Show, Stafford

January: Scottish National Championship Show

AUSTRALIA
Major shows:
Perth Royal Show;
Royal National Capital Poultry Show;
Royal Queensland Show;
Sydney Royal Easter Show

CANADA
November: APA Canadian National Meet; Vernon Pigeon and Poultry Association, British Columbia

CONTINENTAL EUROPE
For details of shows in France, Germany, Holland, etc. and links to other relevant wildfowling European websites, see:
http://volaillepoultry.pagesperso-orange.fr/expositions.html

USA
Major shows:
The Crossroads Show, Indianapolis;
Pacific Northwest Poultry Association Show;
Southern Ohio Poultry Breeders Show, Ohio;
United Poultry Fanciers Show, Iowa

ASSOCIATIONS

BRITAIN
The British Call Duck Club
Website www.thebritishcallduckclub.co.uk

British Waterfowl Association
(contact: Mrs S. Schubert)
PO Box 163
Oxted, Surrey RH8 0WP
Website www.waterfowl.org.uk
Telephone 01892 740212
Email info@waterfowl.org.uk

Call Duck Association UK
Website www.callducks.net

The Domestic Waterfowl Club
Limetree Cottage
Brightwalton, Newbury
Berkshire RG20 7BZ
Website www.domestic-waterfowl.co.uk
Telephone 01488 638014 (evenings)
Email hatcher579@btinternet.com

Indian Runner Club
(contact: Mrs D. Meatyard)
Telephone 01749 812758

Indian Runner Duck Association
Website www.runnerduck.net
Email runnerdux@yahoo.co.uk

Poultry Club
Keeper's Cottage, 40 Benvarden Road
Dervock, Ballymoney
Co. Antrim BT53 6NN
Website www.poultryclub.org
Telephone 02820 741056

Rare Breeds Survival Trust (RBST)
Stoneleigh Park, Nr Kenilworth
Warwickshire CV8 2LG
Website www.rbst.org.uk
Telephone 024 7669 6551
(The RBST currently lists rare-breed chickens,
but plans to extend its list to waterfowl)

Scottish Waterfowl Club
(contact: S. W. Simister)
Website www.scottishwaterfowlclub.co.uk
Telephone 01848 331696

AUSTRALIA
NSW Waterfowl Breeders Association, Inc.
Website www.nswwaterfowl.com

Poultry Stud Breeders and Exhibitors of
Victoria, Australia
Website www.psbev.com.au

South East Queensland Waterfowl
Association, Inc.
Website www.seqwa.net

Victorian Waterfowl Association
Website www.vwa.backyardpoultry.com

USA
American Livestock Breeds Conservancy
PO Box 477
Pittsboro, NC 27312
Website www.albc-usa.org (includes information
on the waterfowl census)

American Poultry Association
PO Box 306
Burgettstown, PA 15021
Website www.amerpoultryassn.com (includes
information on shows)

International Waterfowl Breeders Association
(President: James Konecny)
10219 Heagers Bend Road
Barrington Hills, IL 60102
Website www.iwba.org
Telephone 847 458 4005
Email RoyalOaksFowl@aol.com

PICTURE CREDITS
Fotolia/Stanislav Alekseev: p11
Fotolia/varvara8: p12
Shutterstock/Jeff Gynan: p8

REFERENCES

British Poultry Standards, Sixth Edition, Edited by
Victoria Roberts, Blackwell Publishing in association
with the Poultry Club of Great Britain, 2008

British Waterfowl Standards, Edited by Mike and
Chris Ashton, British Waterfowl Association, 2008

Choosing and Keeping Ducks and Geese,
Liz Wright, Gaia, 2008

Ducks, Geese and Turkeys, Young Farmers'
Club Booklet No. 11, National Federation of Young
Farmers Clubs, 1944

'Runner Ducks', E. A. Taylor, *Country Life,* 1918

Utility Poultry Farming for Australasia,
F. E. A. Gordon, Whitcombe and Tomes United,
New Zealand, 1908

AUTHOR'S ACKNOWLEDGEMENTS

For Mick and Buffy, for their support.

Thanks to *Smallholder* magazine
www.smallholder.co.uk
and *Fancy Fowl* magazine
www.fancyfowl.com

This book is a tribute to duck breeders past
and present, to those who first introduced the
beautiful breeds to their countries, to those who
painstakingly developed new breeds, and to the
people today who take so much pride in – and have
so much knowledge of – these ducks, which are
a living and stunning heritage. Their history is our
history, too.

PUBLISHER'S ACKNOWLEDGEMENTS

*We would like to thank the following organizations
for their help and cooperation in arranging the
photo shoot:*

Special thanks to Mike Hatcher, Chris Parker,
Robert MacDonald, James Baker, Andrew
Wakeham, Dan Wakeham, and also to Graham
Hicks of Waterfowl World, www.waterfowl.co.uk.

ACKNOWLEDGMENTS *continued*

The National Poultry Show
www.poultryclub.org

The Scottish National Poultry Show
www.scottishwaterfowlclub.co.uk

The Domestic Waterfowl Club
www.domestic-waterfowl.co.uk

*We would like to thank all the duck owners and
breeders for their assistance at the photo shoot:*

Indian Runner – American Fawn & White
Mike Hatcher
Orpington – Buff Graham Hicks
Abacot Ranger Graham Hicks
Muscovy – Chocolate James Baker
Indian Runner – White Paul Meatyard
Aylesbury Graham Hicks
Magpie – Dun & White Graham Hicks
Blue Swedish A. P. Stanway
Indian Runner – Trout Team Wakeham
Rouen Clair Graham Hicks
Crested – White J. Christopher
Saxony Paul Meatyard
Miniature Silver Appleyard Graham Hicks
Pekin Graham Hicks
Indian Runner – Chocolate M. Winston
Miniature Silver Appleyard Danny McCarthy
Miniature Crested – Coloured Graham Hicks
Hook Bill Mr A. P. Stanway
Indian Runner – Fawn Mike Hatcher
Black East Indian Mr D. M. Durie
Silver Bantam Graham Hicks
Muscovy – Black & White Graham Hicks
Silver Appleyard Danny McCarthy
Cayuga Charles Holtom
Campbell – Khaki Graham Hicks
Call – Yellow Belly A. Davies
Bali – Coloured Graham Hicks
Call – Black K. Williamson
Miniature Crested – Coloured Graham Hicks
Indian Runner – Fawn & White P. Birch
Welsh Harlequin – Light Russell Lee Jones
Rouen Graham Hicks
Overberg Graham Hicks
Campbell – White Peter Hayford
Muscovy – Black Team Wakeham
Indian Runner – Black Mike Hatcher
Call – Apricot Chris Millward
Call – White Chris Millward
Campbell – Dark Graham Hicks
Bali – White R. Sadler

INDEX